From

*What do I wish you, on this special day?*
*Time enough to soak in a scented bath, to reach the last chapter of that book you've been trying for months to finish, to experiment with a new and glamorous hairstyle? The choice is yours – and who deserves the luxury of choice more than a lovely, loving and hard-pressed Mother?*

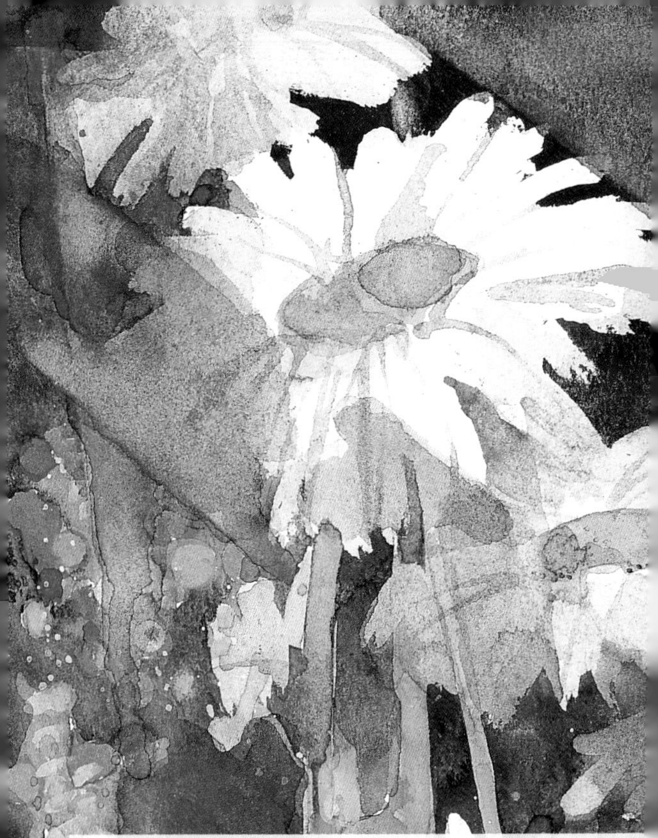

*To a lovely mother, Happy Mother's Day!*
*These are my hopes on this, your own*
*special day.*
*That your health stays fine,*
*your mood remains sunny, your friends*
*and family love you lots*
*– and that all those ambitions put on*
*hold move several steps further*
*toward achievement!*

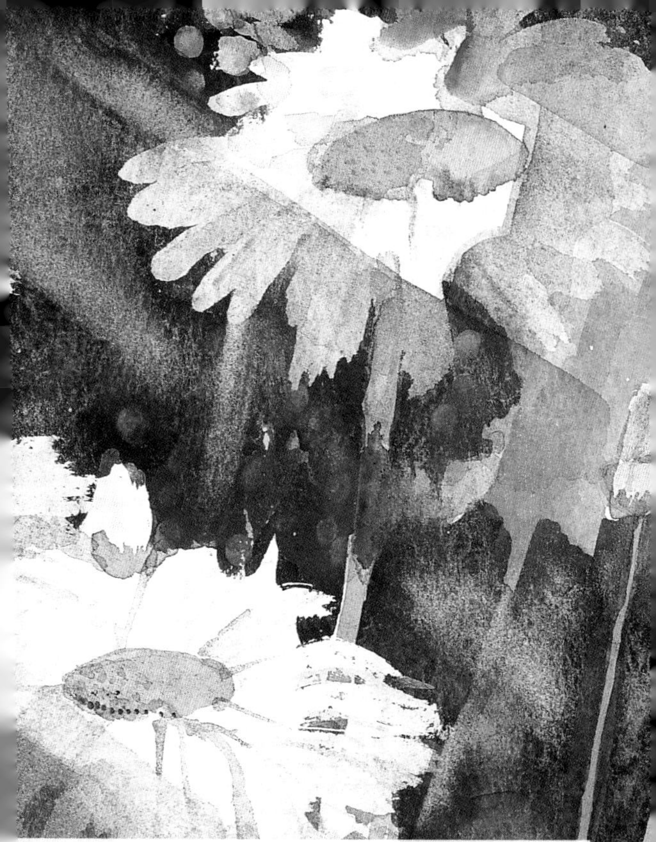

*In the language of flowers,*
*bluebells symbolize Constancy,*
*honeysuckle stands for Generous*
*and Devoted Affection, the rose*
*means Love, and the oak leaf*
*is a sign of Bravery.*
*Guess what's in the bouquet*
*I want to send to you, on this*
*your special day!*

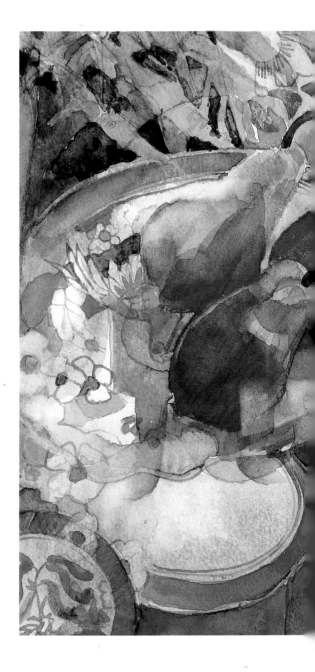

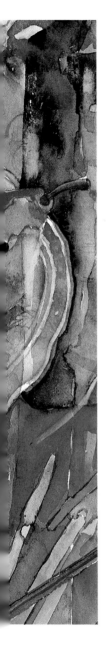

*Thank you for keeping me safe
within yourself so long,
sheltering me in my most secret
life, releasing me at last to
independence. Giving me
welcome, teaching me love.
Caring for me through sickness,
tears, tantrums and stubborn,
sullen silences. Believing in me
– even at the edges of despair.*

PAM BROWN, b.1928

*Whatever beauty or poetry is to
be found in my little book is
owing to your interest in and
encouragement of all my efforts
from the first to the last; and if
ever I do anything to be proud
of, my greatest happiness will
be that I can thank you for
that, as I may do for all the
good there is in me; and I shall
be content to write if it gives
you pleasure.*

LOUISA MAY ALCOTT
(1832-1888), TO HER
MOTHER

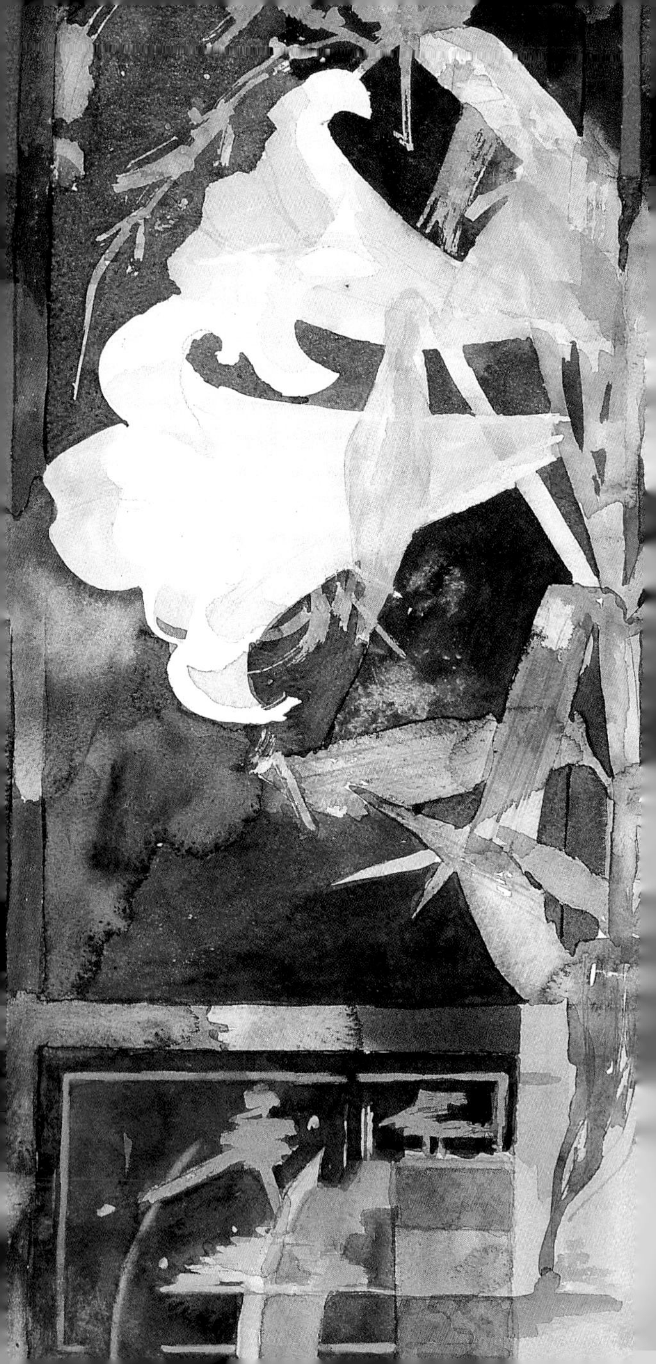

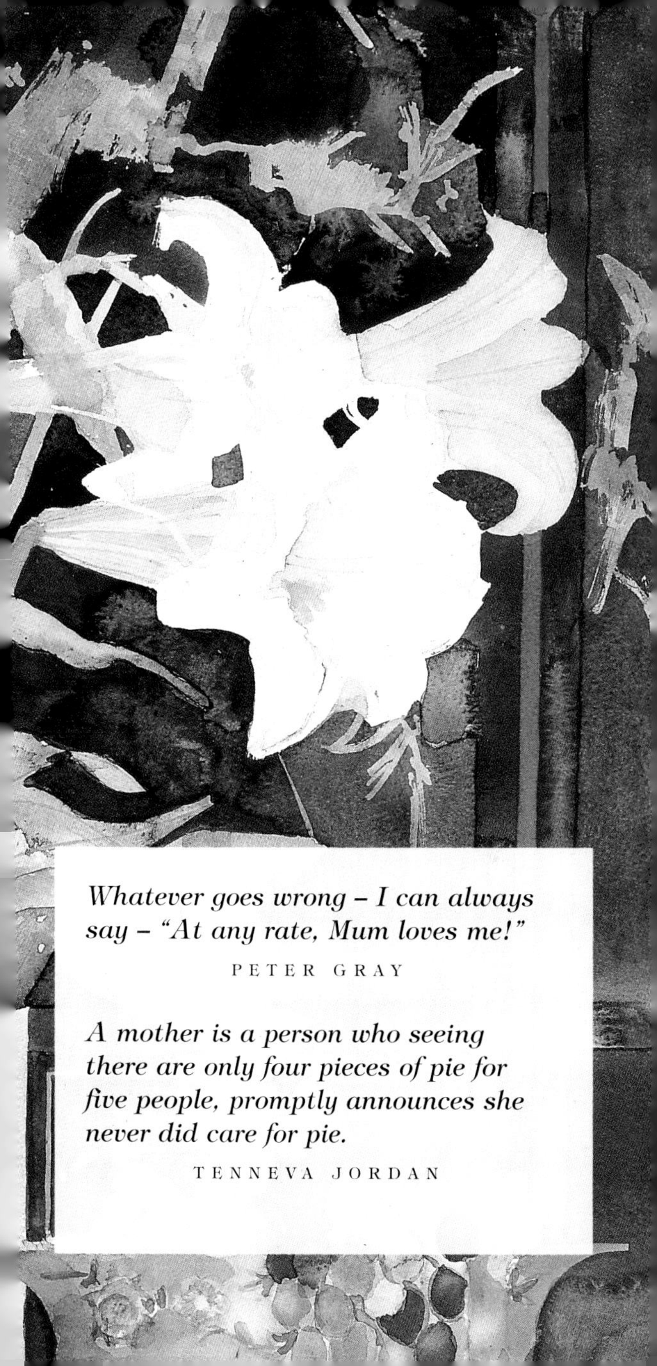

*Whatever goes wrong – I can always say – "At any rate, Mum loves me!"*

PETER GRAY

*A mother is a person who seeing there are only four pieces of pie for five people, promptly announces she never did care for pie.*

TENNEVA JORDAN

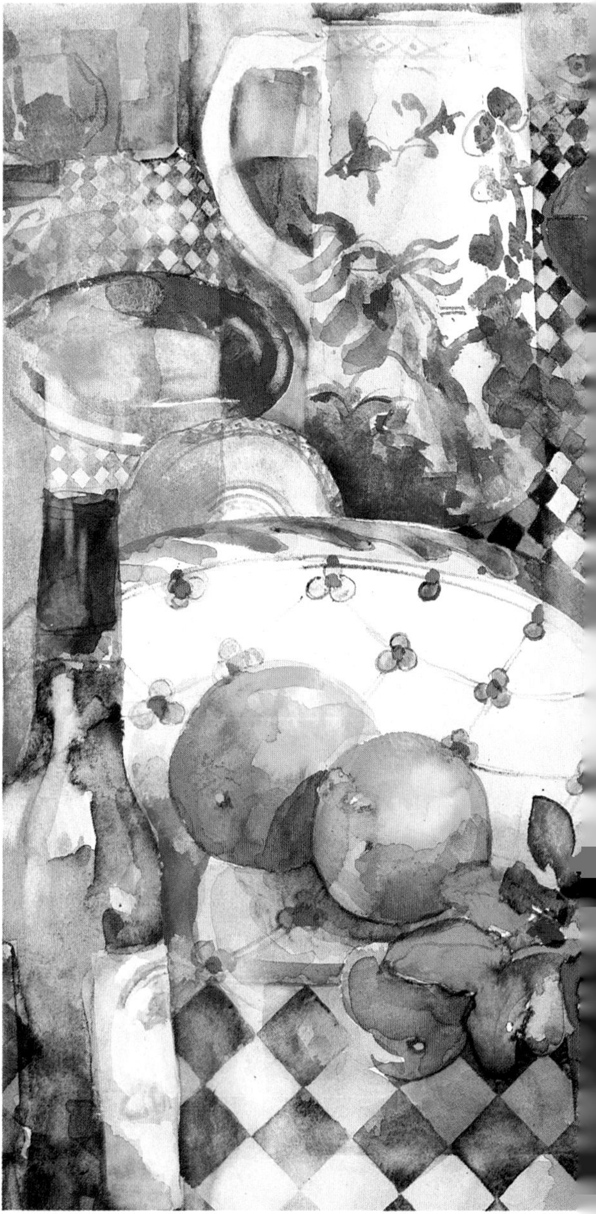

*Whatever success comes to me seems incomplete because you are so often not at my side to be glad with me.*

HELEN KELLER (1880-1968)

*I assure you that I have never received one of your dear letters without regretting, with tears in my eyes, that I am separated from such a tender and good mother, and though I am happy enough here, I still ardently wish I could return to see my dear, my very dear family....*

QUEEN MARIE ANTOINETTE, TO HER MOTHER

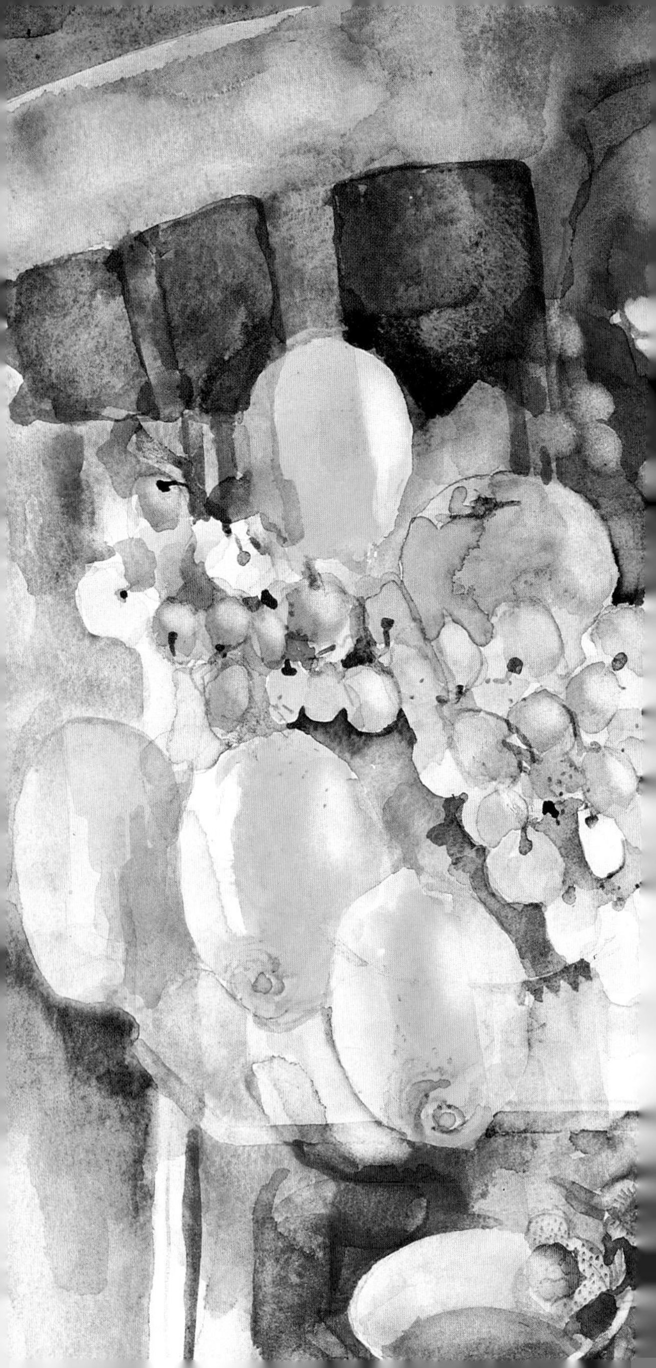

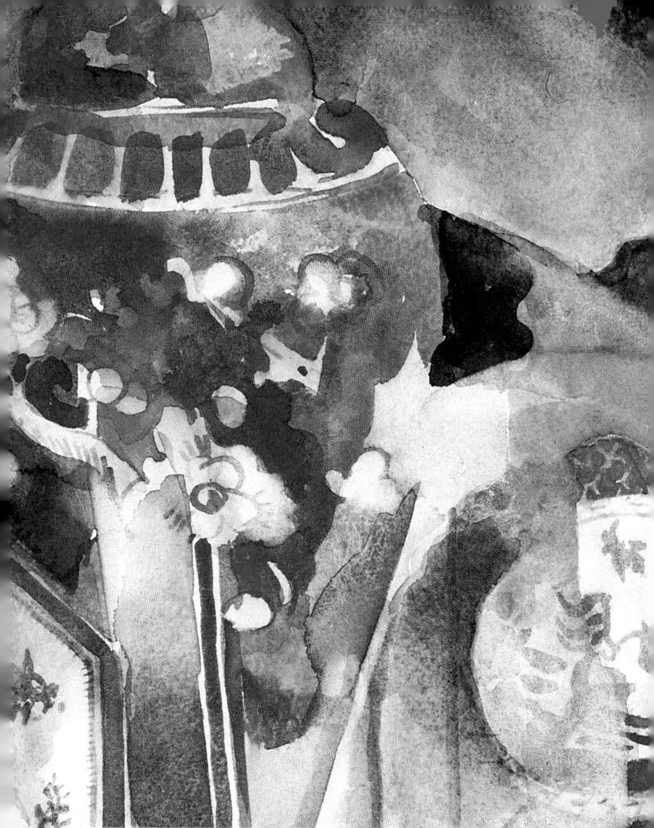

*I have pushed hard against some of the rules of the "good daughter" and learned to really hear the message my mother has given me all my life: "I will be with you always." As in forever, into the eternal hereafter, no matter what.*

REBECCA WALKER,
DAUGHTER OF ALICE WALKER

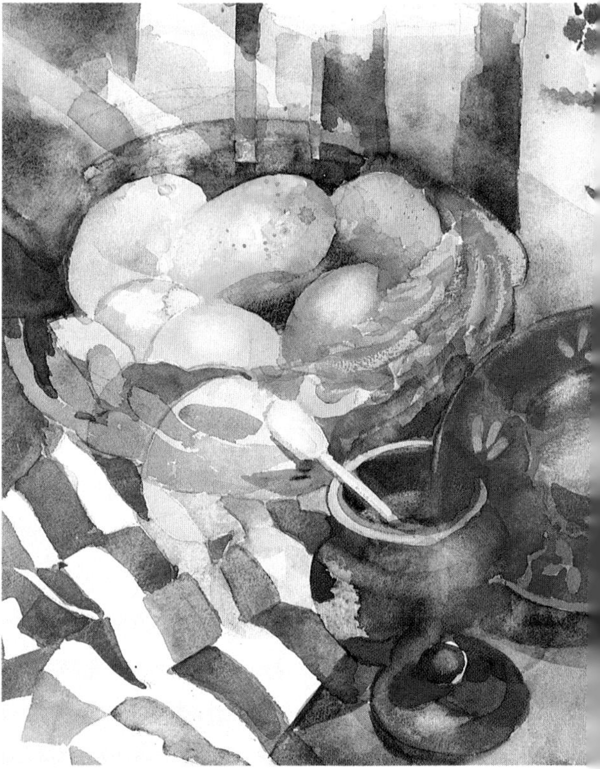

*When you [have]... a close relationship with your mother, who can compete? The comfort, the championing, the humour and familiarity, built for so long upon each other, is a hard game to beat. To trust an unknown quantity with a physical and emotional intimacy unknown outside childhood, you have to be*

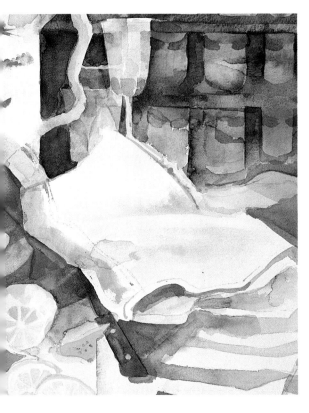

*brave. Far easier not to trust. But when you have a good and close relationship with your mother, it allows and encourages others. It's against suffocating exclusivity, it breeds belief and trust, it wants its child to grow kind, honest, strong, happy, graceful and independent.*

SOPHIE PARKIN, b.1961

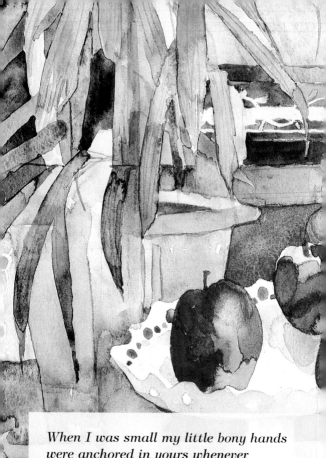

When I was small my little bony hands
were anchored in yours whenever
danger threatened – wherever there was
something grand to see – whenever we were
scampering towards a new adventure.
Now they meet as older hands – as those of
companions and friends.
But holding a lifetime of loving in their touch

PAM BROWN, b.1928

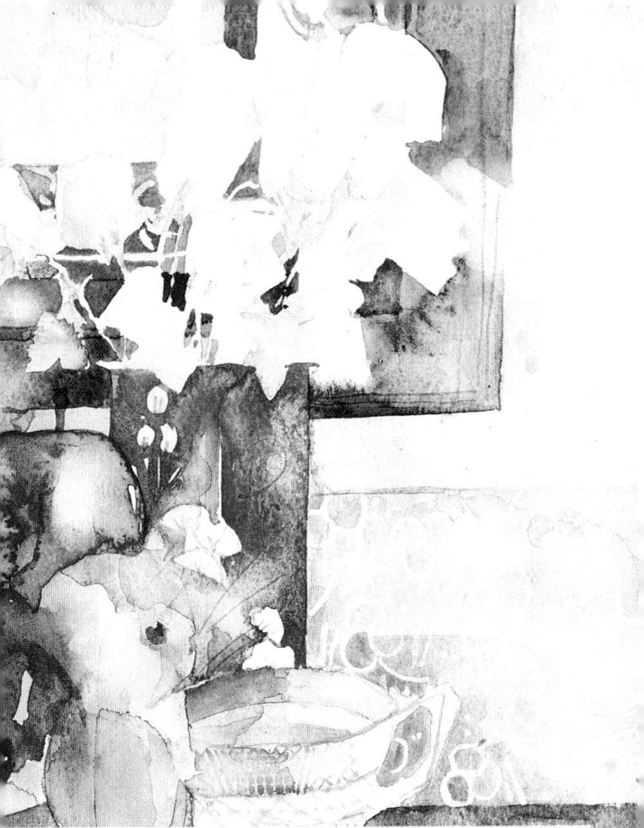

*Even as adults we sometimes catch ourselves calling for "mommy." As if mommies could really soothe and erase the pain and fear and make everything better, just the way they were once able to do when we believed in their omniscience, their eternal and unconditional love and power.*

JOAN HULL

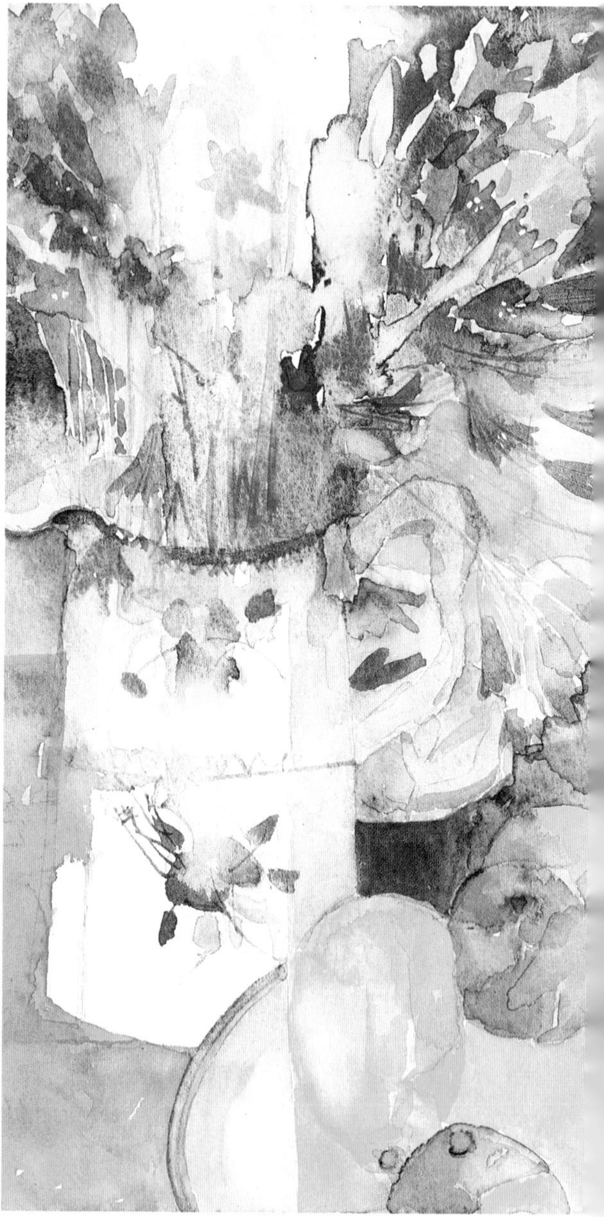

*The years, as they come, every one, deepen my gratitude to you, as I better understand the significance of life, and every one adds to the affection that never was small.*

WALTER HINES PAGE,
IN A LETTER TO HIS
MOTHER

*The image of the mother who sacrifices all her dreams for her husband and her children is inspirational – for the husband and the kids.*
*But you? You deserve your dreams. You deserve your chance.*
*You deserve your accolade. We're right behind you.*
*You're a wonderful mother – but you're a wonderful woman too.*

PAM BROWN, b.1928

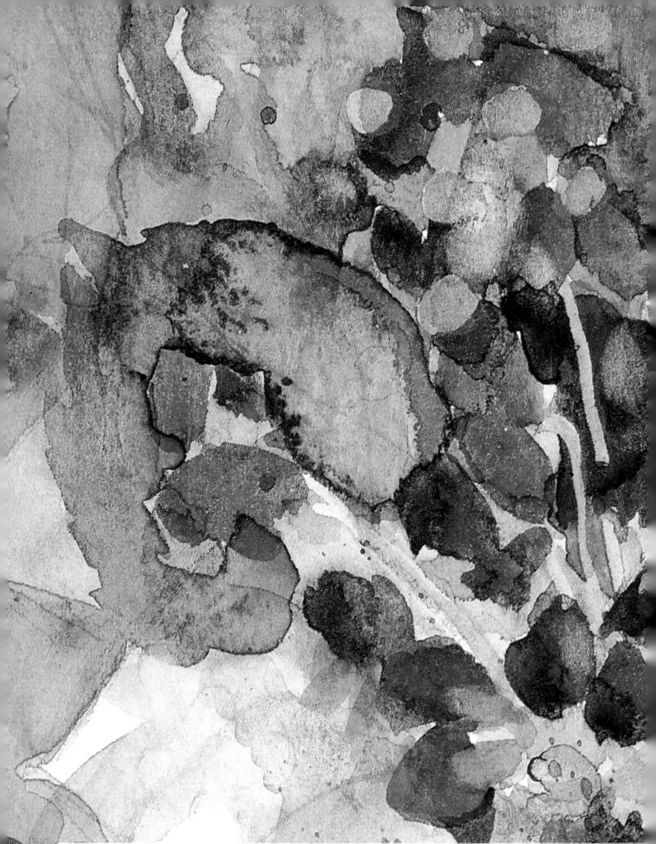

*A mother is someone to confide in, laugh with, cry with and go to when you need advice. She's someone who knows you better than anyone else does – or probably ever will.*

NANCY REAGAN, b.1923

*... when a child needs a mother to talk to, nobody else but a mother will do.*

ERICA JONG, b.1942

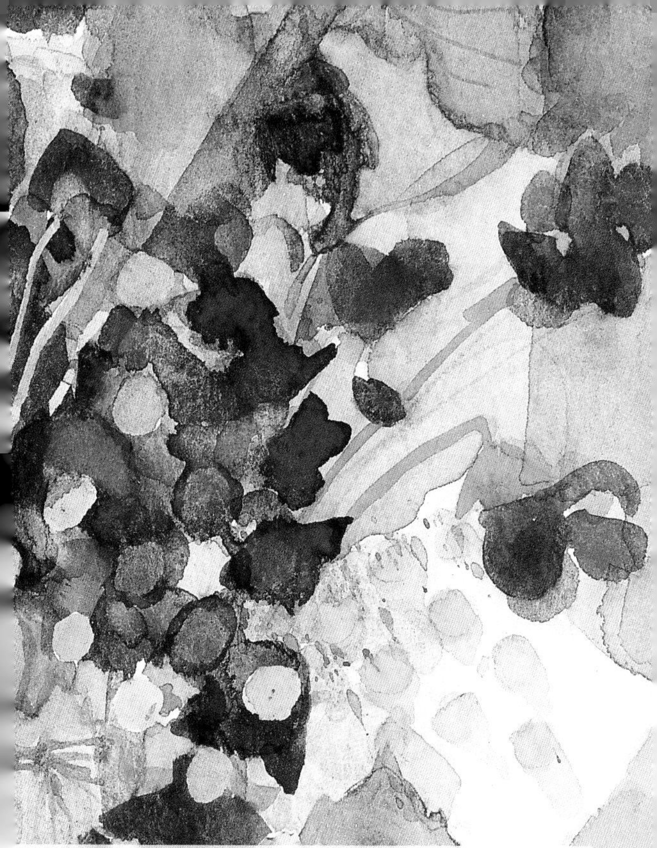

*Mothers mix a brew of scents.*
*Polish and disinfectant, talcum powder, baked apples. Potting compost. Oranges and lilac. Burnt toast. Clean linen.*
*It met us at the door. Warm. Safe. Home.*

PAM BROWN, b.1928

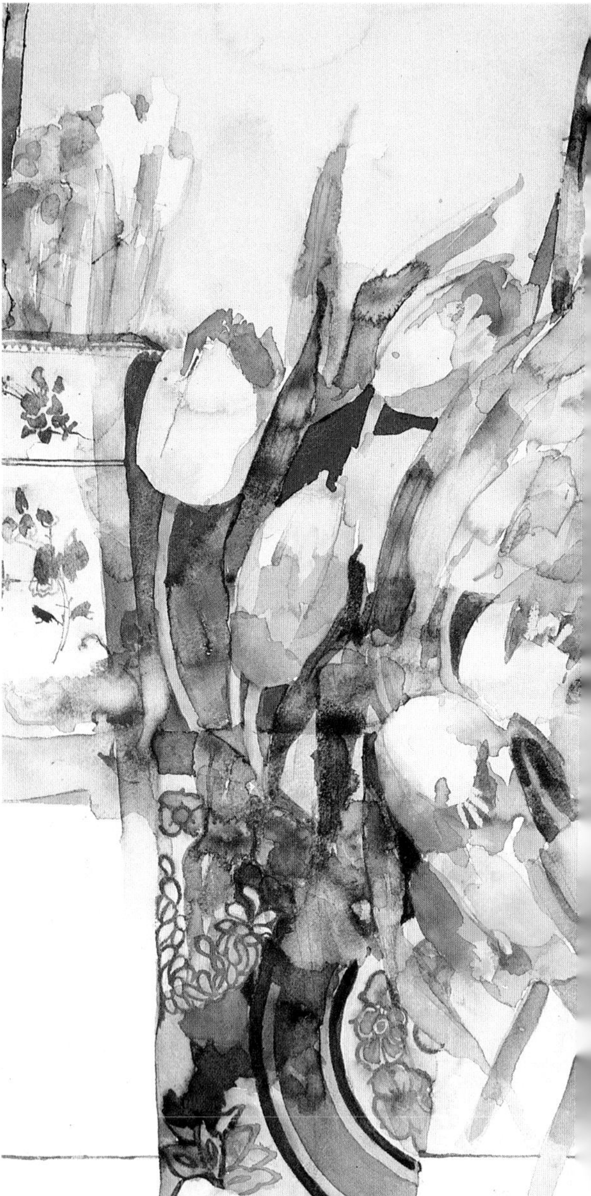

*She is roses, and London gardens, she is wartime movies, and Frank Sinatra songs, she is Italy and France, and China tea. She is soaked through everything I see. I look at my face in the mirror, at my mannerisms, the veins in my hands, and realise she will always be with me.*

HARRIET WALTER, FROM "*MOTHERS – BY DAUGHTERS*"

*I feel total love, trust, warmth and joy between us. The serenity she has now found after the turbulent life she'd led for so long is only what she deserves. It benefits us all.*
*"How lucky we are," she said to me on Mother's Day surrounded by red, purple and orange tulips, "that we've both reached this point so early on in life."*
*"Yes, aren't we," I said embracing her. "Happy Mother's Day, Mum."*

SOPHIE PARKIN, b.1961

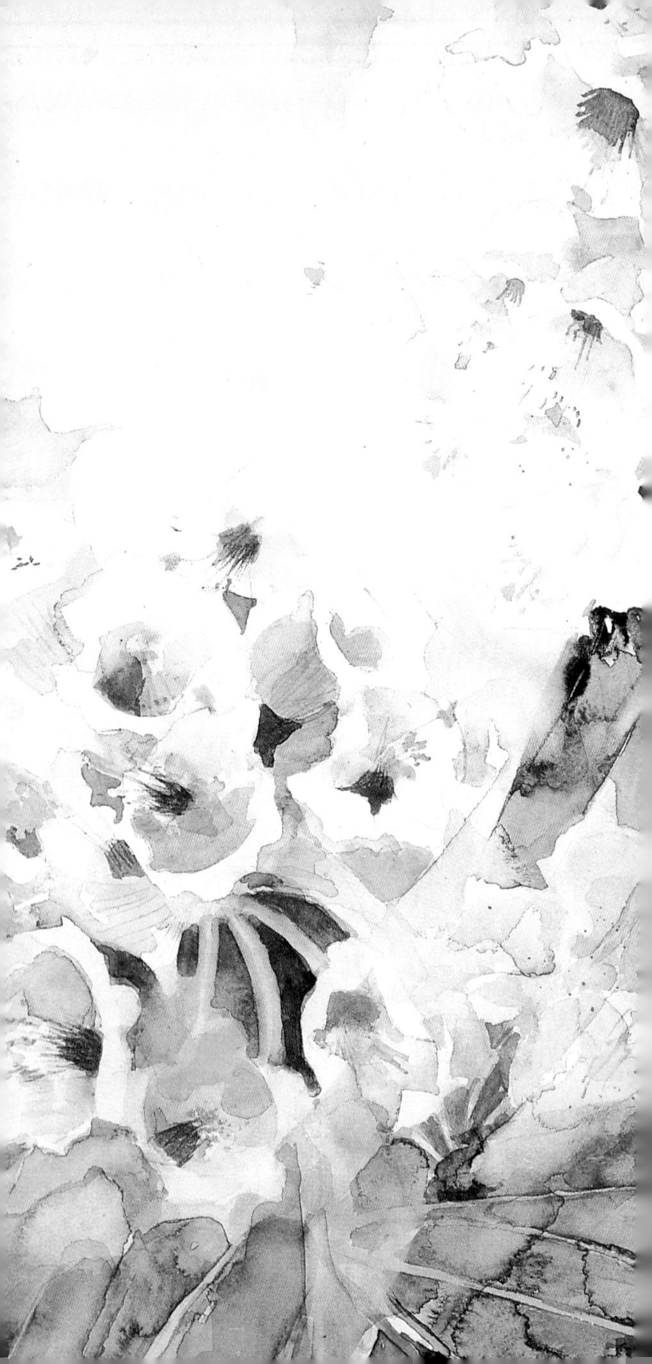

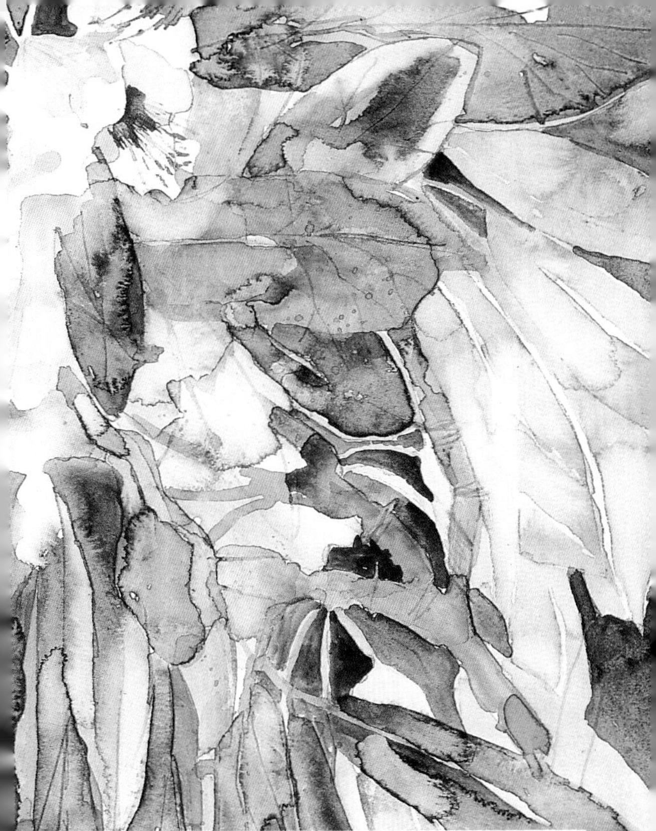

*Because you believe in me – I can believe in myself.*

CHARLOTTE GRAY

*Houses and hotels, huts and tents and sailing boats – all can be my home while I am there. For you gave me love and the certainty that I can cope everywhere.*

PAM BROWN, b.1928

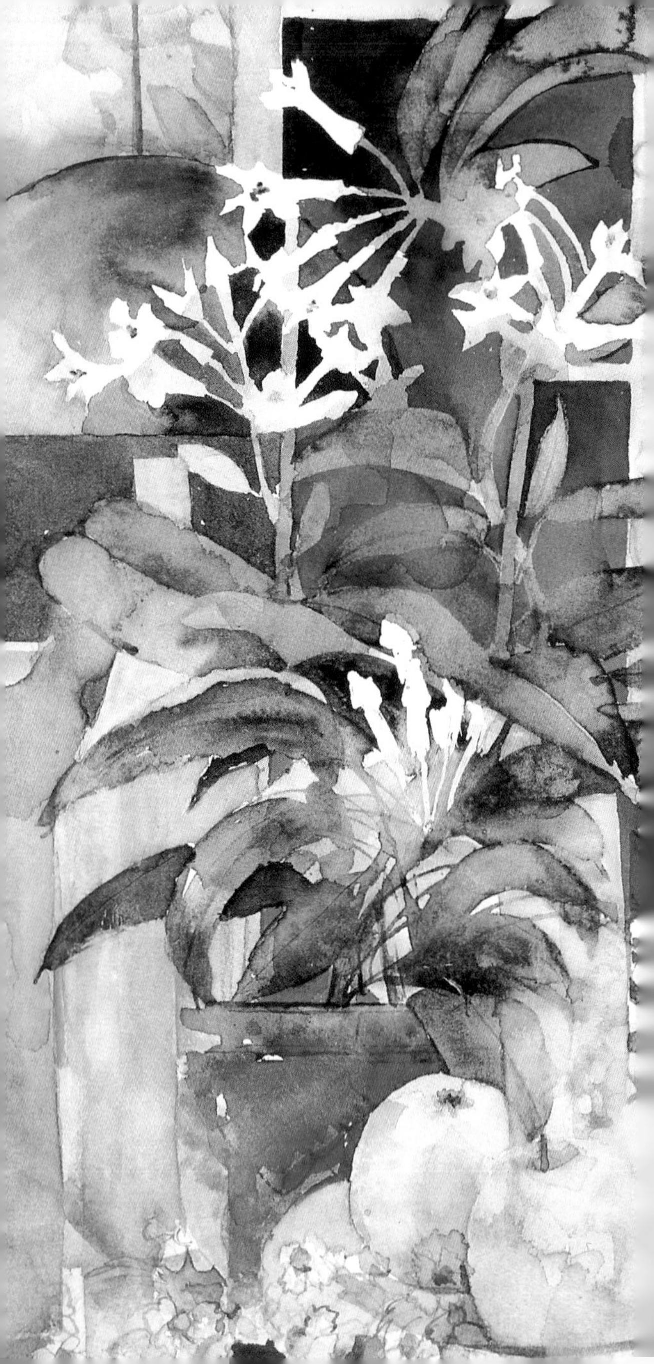